Wine Away Our Cares

The Flavors of Friendship

words by Sheri Wall

art by Ilona Stuijt

To my special friends

Thank you for welcoming me into your circle with open arms, cheerful hearts, and chilled spirits.

S.W.

A MATTER OF RHYME

A Matter of Rhyme
www.amatterofrhyme.com

Printed in the United States of America
2nd edition
ISBN: 978-1-7330943-9-9

To

friends everywhere

and the

memories they share

Sheri Wall

Girl time we need
Sublime indeed
We dish, we bond, we bare.

Our souls exposed
Yet this we know
We'll wine away our cares.

We pour, we drink
We smile, we think
Secrets and dreams we share.
We laugh, we cry
We sip, we sigh
Reflection beyond compare.

Moscato

With fizz and the flavor of peach
We've been known to pack some
For a trip to the beach.

Rosé

Such beauty with a delicate blush
While relaxing on pillows
We spill our first crush.

Rose

Sangria

A blend adding fruit to infuse
We lift up our voices
As inhibitions we lose.

Chardonnay

Aged in oak so smooth and refined
We savor its essence
With dinner and unwind.

Char

Merlot

In French means "little blackbird"
If we drink just enough
Our fears will be cured.

Prosecco

Champagne's sparkling Italian cousin
At brunch in our stemware
When sampling pastries and muffins.

Mulled Wine

With reds and just the right spice
A warm mug after skiing
No need to think twice.

Cabernet Sauvignon

So red and so bold
Just come as you are
Let the good times unfold.

We pour, we drink
We smile, we think
Secrets and dreams we share
We laugh, we cry
We sip, we sigh
Friendship beyond compare.

I have fond memories of...

Some favorite wines are...

True friendship is...

Some fabulous wineries are...

Remember the time...

I dream about...

The vintage of wine is the year in which the grapes were grown.

Sometimes the word crush is also used to mean harvest.

Averaging 75 grapes in a cluster, one cluster of grapes makes one glass of wine.

Many wines can be found in a non-alcoholic variety.

There is at least one winery in each of the 50 United States and in virtually every country of the world.

Red wine gets lighter with age, and white wine gets darker with age.

Wine is stored laying down to prevent the cork from drying and shrinking.

Wine glasses come in eighteen different types with a shape and style unique to each wine.

There are about ten thousand wine grape varieties worldwide.

The five "S" steps to tasting wine are see, swirl, smell, sip, and swallow.

Sheri Wall is an award-winning children's book author residing in Central Texas. After being inspired by some dear friends, she decided to write a book that showcased their love of community and wine while integrating the fun, playful rhythms for which A Matter of Rhyme is known.

In addition to learning about and sampling delectable wines, Sheri enjoys cooking, eating, decorating, bargain hunting, and being active.

See her children's books and contact Sheri at amatterofrhyme.com.

Ilona Stuijt is a traveling illustrator from the Netherlands. She has worked on over a dozen books for children and adults in collaboration with Sheri and other writers from all over the world.

You can find more of her work on lankyartist.com.